M000220869

case sensitive

ahsahta press

The New Series

number 14

case sensitive

Kate Greenstreet

AHSAHTA PRESS

Boise State University • Boise • Idaho • 2006

Ahsahta Press, Boise State University
Boise, Idaho 83725
http://ahsahtapress.boisestate.edu

Copyright © 2006 by Kate Greenstreet
Printed in the United States of America
Cover design by M & K Greenstreet
Photos by Max Greenstreet
Book design by Janet Holmes
First printing September 2006
ISBN: 0-916272-89-3
ISBN-13: 978-0-916272-89-0

Library of Congress Cataloging-in-Publication Data

Greenstreet, Kate.
case sensitive / Kate Greenstreet.
    p. cm. -- (The new series ; no.14)
Includes bibliographical references and index.
ISBN-13: 978-0-916272-89-0 (pbk. : alk. paper)
I. Title. II. Series: New series (Ahsahta Press) ; no. 14.

PS3607.R4666C37 2006
811'.6--dc22

                        2006005227

ACKNOWLEDGMENTS

Thanks to the editors of the print and online journals in which some of these poems first appeared: *26 , Bird Dog, can we have our ball back?, Carve, Conduit, CutBank, Diagram, Fascicle, Free Verse, MiPOesias, No Tell Motel, Octopus, Rhino, Saint Elizabeth Street, the tiny, Traverse, Word For/Word,* and *Xantippe.*

"Learning the Language" and "Bridge" also appear in *Learning the Language,* a chapbook published by Etherdome Press in 2005.

"dusting for prints" also appears in the anthology *DIAGRAM.2,* published by New Michigan Press in 2006.

Contents

Great Women of Science

Many things about the story are puzzling.
The women cooking, the men

swimming in the sea.
I believe we need light

inside the body.
Her necklace is

sparkling, see?
See the sparkle lines?

Wood into gold, "this diamond, this
poetry I speak of"—

I always wished I had a different voice.
Do you remember playing "having a baby" on your porch?

Taking turns
as the groaning, screaming woman.

And as the nurse
who brought the doll. It gets more like this.

The roof began to collapse. I realized
I couldn't reach the door.
Is it fall
or winter? There seem to be bright colored leaves on the trees.
Can we meet?
Do you believe in fate?

Can't tell you how your phrase "the letter from a ghost"
makes me feel. Recognized.
If "upset" could also mean "relieved."
(When a ghost is seen.)

I'll do my family tree for you, but mine
is no different from most.
The goose so proud, the burro
so woebegone. By the way,
I was kind of hoping there are lots of things you didn't say yet.

After a decade away, she revisited the place where she'd grown up.

A letter was delivered five years late.

"I don't know why I felt under the mattress, but something was there."

I called your house but you weren't home. No one there knew the line about the pilgrims (you would've). The furnace clicks like Morse code but never kicks in. You can cash that check now.

meant to be?
where was I going—
pulling out parts
from a string:
perhaps
one day.

the unsatisfied, their souls
in peril—for grass,
the dead part they like so much,
the blue light:
come to the last,
I had to say no.

Once mentally created, they had life,
didn't realize they were dead, and wouldn't just
disappear when their presence

became uncomfortable for him.
One night, while he was at a meeting,
I ripped out everything: shelves, cabinets, wallboard.

When he came back,
he helped me finish the job and
clean up. How do these feelings change?

"I believed that you had broken my heart."

Day after day was
deeply involved. Unperturbed,
the young king continued to burn.

To make his way,
for tomorrow.

We often found ourselves broke and
disoriented. "Now comes the science," she said.

9 p.m. on a Tuesday, the laundromat's closed. The last warm night of October. A few crickets. The last ferry comes in, so slowly. The fortuneteller climbs up a ladder with a roller in her hand, in a hot pink shirt. She seems young to know so much. The door is open. She's been painting the inside of her place bright white. The outside of the storefront they did last week: a surprising golden ochre. The streets are dark. One open restaurant, empty. Ropes slapping hollow metal masts, occasionally. Not much wind.

What's the appeal of a mystery? Someone is looking for something, actively.

Sound of scraping. Then the slapping sound of
application. (Still trying to look nice.)

Still want to tell: how many coats I put on.
How long it took me to get numb.

One thing that ghosts have in common:
they always want to tell you how they died.

They're Latin, they're technical, nailed
to the door. Thus:

endless confession.
Everything changed.

Hours in a
contrite position.

Nor could I believe I pleased Him with my labor
(hand set, open to arrest).

To prove our existence, it was essential to isolate.
I spoke of you several times today.

My son, my brother, my husband, my father—
that we were alive at the same time.

I was in love with the idea of a friend.
The opposite of magic.

The basic
conditional is
the standard *if.*

Faith
(the step we took)
is her middle name. Love the leaf.

I have faith.
Help my lack of faith.

It happens all of a sudden. Even after all the planning, and the packing. You're in the car, you're driving, you're watching the signs.

I didn't want to stop. But when I dropped off again, I took the next exit, toward a kind of complex I could see—big diner, gas station, long row of tiny motel rooms, half a neon cowboy.

I was nervous, but nobody looked at me twice. And by the time I'd pulled up to number fifteen, and got my mother's good suitcase and the rest of my tunafish sandwiches in on the bed, I felt pretty good. I locked the door, both locks, and unwrapped another sandwich. And drank a glass of water from the tap, with a toast to my escape.

"it comes in bullets,
in jets
and that's the modern way"

"Well, we're the long range people"

"approves or—discards—this is murder—
you see...during the years—thirty—"
"I wouldn't ask, as you say."

"too tired to lift it."

"I could have delved
into deeper things but
one can't risk—"

[ ]

"—talking clears the air
and brings out half a laugh
...we poor beings

with what we think...

[D]irectly
that's our best way"
"not just for me

but the world. And while we live."[1]

By the third day of driving it's easier—much—to eat alone in truck stops and stop at motels (to consider the third) by myself. Hardly cry at all. I write a little while I wait for my food. Starting over—the idea—is a lot like the idea of mental health. ("When you woke up, was it there?")

After the fire, or the accident, she returns to the town where they last all lived as a family. An unknown relative dies, leaving her a huge old house with a troubled history.

Disappearing objects, a surprising document. There was a chance that tragedy might be averted. Children were missing. Adults misunderstood the signs.

Thinking about mysteries—the books called mysteries—as I drive past town after town, "the middle of nowhere." Every morning I wake up alone, again, in something like the same strange room, take a shower, re-pack, and get back into the car.

It was surprisingly easy to leave. Even to keep secret the storage space and my trips to it. I take as proof of how invisible I was, the way he didn't notice things were gone.

"Matter." And "thought."
Both must.

These dreams—
old ice, to protect what?

There is an obstacle.
("lifted")

The body
is the last world.

My mother taught me.
She had her life by dates.
We did the kitchen pink.
"Reach beyond what you know."

Some ideas were:
Stuff on shelves.
Empty shelves.

I was icing this cake for her,
but it was crumbling
underneath.
(It wasn't a very good-looking cake.)

You say
you want to do something.
Or, you say: What *can* I do?[2]

There is an obstacle, called
"safe passage."

"There are places that we go—to keep from going somewhere else.
Well, partly, we've been waiting our whole lives—"

There were millions.

There were all those years.

notes

1. This section (from "it comes" to "we live.") is composed of phrases from the letters of Lorine Niedecker, quoted in Jenny Penberthy, *Niedecker and the Correspondence with Zukofsky, 1931-1970* (Cambridge University Press, 1993), 94 (to Kenneth Cox), 96-99 (to Cid Corman). Penberthy describes "the pervasive empty brackets sign [ ]" used by Zukofsky and Niedecker in their correspondence as "a signal of deep caring for which words dare not and need not be found." Reprinted with the permission of Cambridge University Press.

2. "You say you want to do something. Or you say: what can I do?" Agnes Martin, in Mary Lance's video portrait, *Agnes Martin: With My Back to the World* (New Deal Films, Inc. 2002).

[SALT]

When sodium, an unstable metal that can suddenly burst into flame, reacts with a deadly poisonous gas known as chlorine, it becomes the staple food sodium chloride... from the only family of rocks eaten by humans.[1]

1 [is abundant on and deep within the earth]

Mostly I'm alone but sometimes my mother is asleep, in another room. Last night we were sleeping in the same bed beside a giant window. I heard talking and went to investigate. I heard a door click shut, a lock turned. The TV was on in the other room, and the milk and the salt were on the counter. I realized that the people who ran the place, who could lock the door from the other side, had been in our apartment, using our stuff and hanging out. I went to tell my mother. Then I noticed the big window was open a crack. I could close it, but the lock was broken.

2 [was known to have been made]

She was on the medicine for grief.
"Even if they don't die, it doesn't help much."

Grit of salt around her chair.
Basically, a question you have to ask yourself.

Can you shut the eye with something in it and continue?
"Most commonly, this transformation takes

the form of disappearances
of persons."[2]

What do we share
that can help us?

"In the very distant
universe,

Objects
even older than light."[3]

Manifold
destiny. A kind of song. Escape

with what you are. Walking,
talking, for a thousand miles...

"Some may not need gold, but who
does not need salt?"[4] And sometime after,

felt the need to write.
Wherewith will it be salted?

Why bring it up again? Red eyes,
read for meaning.

The buried ring, marked map, "the consolation
of religion."

Things go together because they *are* together.
It's a challenge to the spirit that cleans the spirit.

Snow on the cold side
of the fence.

Isn't that the definition
of sense?

3 [on icy streets makes winter travel safe]

What would I do if I were serious?
Most people have been dead for more than twenty years.

I was getting my car fixed, waiting, and
a man, an older man who seemed to have a hole in his throat said
Hi.
Remember me?

Everybody wants a simple answer.

4 [did not provide an easy life]

Little pigs lose their intuition around the age of 3, become opaque, and forget how to feed themselves. They'll just stay where someone puts them, and fade into the background where they are because they've lost their special light.

We heard the songs about it. They can recover (the songs said) if they can survive.

"A flat denial? Just to start with?"[5]

What makes us alive wants to change.

5 [breaks spells]

Nothing was known about the refining of salt, and it was difficult to tell the difference between salt and sand on the shores of the sea.[6]

It's white. It starts to come down.

The sky gets white but it's darker. The whole sky is gray.

Wind. There's wind, often.

It's white and dark at the same time. It can accumulate.

Uniodized. It tastes the same, I'd try to remind her.

The light changes and it gets more white. And a feeling in the air—of moisture, and the smell. Not salt. The smell of seaweed maybe? I don't know.

If you had a cup of ocean water, I don't think that it would smell. Is it the plants of the sea? Is it the animals of the sea? I really don't know. There's just a feeling of freedom. Everything opens.

The tears themselves? It's like losing your balance.

I've tasted them.

It used to drive me crazy when my mother would lick her tears away. I couldn't look, it made me sick.

When I was little, it was scary. When you get knocked down. It rolls you around, the water gets up your nose, and it's so sandy! And I was always being tortured by my brothers—with the sand crabs and everything in my bathing suit.

But later it was better. I couldn't swim. But I couldn't see why people make such a big deal about that anyway—I mean, what's "swimming," in the ocean? It's a tumultuous force! The waves come and lift you up... it's fun. It was romantic sometimes, you'd be out there with a boy. It isn't so good afterwards. When you dry off.

One is sharp, the other is deceptive. One brings something out, one covers it up. Salt is like the truth and sugar is niceness. Salt brings out the flavor. Well, if you put too much of anything in, that'll ruin it.

Sharp. Like with a point. It's intelligent, it's pure. They used it as a medicine. They'd put a grain of salt into a tooth that had a toothache. One grain... those must've been awfully big grains. You can use it to treat all kinds of things: sprains, toothaches, poison ivy. You can gargle with salt, if you have a sore throat. You get the feeling it might kill germs.

They're white. Or gray. Light colored, like the moon. People make movies out there because it feels like the moon. We had a picnic out there once. You made me a really good sandwich. And maybe another time we were there it was cold.

Salt is ordinary.

People say that pepper's more exciting. She's nice. She's supposedly nice. I don't like her. She was the renowned beauty in her family. The one who was constantly praised by the father as beautiful. Strawberry blonde, it's called. I need space.

Affection. Love. To make things. Time to think. The outside. The outdoors. I need salt. I don't know if all mammals do. But people do.

Frank. Frank eats a lot of salt. He's sharp, he can bring out the flavor. Frank's a good addition. If you were having a party, you'd want Frank there—he'd help. And my grandmother comes to mind, just about cooking.

I guess I think of Frank and my grandmother—not because they're such great truth tellers, but they were more known for their sharpness.

In what form—spilled?

Doesn't spilling it mean bad luck?

Did we get enough? Will we go back?

Pillar of salt. She turned. They had to leave the city.

The city was on fire. It was on fire because it was wicked. They were all told not to look back, but she did. And because of this disobedience, she was turned—into a pillar of salt.

Some people say she looked back because she didn't care what God said, she just missed her rich life. But some people say she turned because that was her home.

It was her home, and it was on fire.

She didn't exist anymore. That was it. Nothing happened to her. She wasn't mentioned again. Except as a warning.

6 [was openly sold on the streets]

No food in the house. Mandelstam went around to the neighbors to try to get something for his guest's dinner. Later, while police rummaged through his papers, that solitary egg still lay on the table untouched. "Suddenly Akhmatova said that M. should eat something before he left, and she held out the egg to him."[7] Who cracked the egg? Who peeled away the shell? He sat down and ate it, with some salt.

7 [raises the boiling point]

She's just there.
What do you mean "What's the deal?"
She's sleeping.
You can spend a long time not doing something.
To lean towards. Also, take care of.

There'll be something.
That's how it was last time.
You start by breaking it down.

It just stinks.
It's the order,
in a sentence.

We expect the words to *come* to us,
in a certain order.
I don't know the answer.
I was young.

It was essential to keep my mother going.
I'm not trying to be hidden, but it's natural.
A story has to leave out nearly everything or nobody can follow it.

8 [will become rock hard but never lose its taste]

A funeral. I had to speak. The words just came.

There were so many dead.

Even as we were burying them, no one was sure who was who.

Everyone was saying what they'd take, if they could only take one thing.

The men would be allowed two things, and nobody knew why.

9 [when used, loses itself]

"What about the tall coat,
and the little coat?"[8]

We see the house where she is
means land, field, ground.

When you touch them,
I feel how hard they're working.

If I were serious?
We are the salt

of the earth.
But if the salt have lost his savour?

"The following names, which occur
over and over…"

10 [has been used to seed clouds]

They say the color of our dead skin matters.
They say we get the help we need.

As Kids We Played on the Paths They Cut. It was a murder mystery.
But instead of a lot of suspects, there were a lot of psychic detectives.

One was just an alive arm. Just the arm was a being.
It took to me, and I wore it then, like a scarf.

11 [can only be safely handled with the middle 2 fingers]

Not thinking about it won't work.
When certain foods will remind you of
certain cruelties.

Salt deprived, he could die and never feel the desire
for salt. This is common,
even fated.

"Bread and salt, a blessing and its
preservation…"[9] Crusts
on the plate represented:

we're doing enough for each other.
I don't know why. But, after that,
one of us might say: "I remembered the crusts."

12 [represents union]

Snow came and covered the house. Wind blew the snow.
She was only waiting secretly for the moment she could again
become herself.[10]

13 [did not originate in the pools where it was found]

I'm going to say it's clouds. Or rain.
You'd be thinking—
about the end of your life. Somewhat.
And also—
the things you'd care about

would be different than the people you knew.
These are harder, I think.
It's just a feeling that we have—the desire to go deeper.
No, in fact, I often don't, and other people do.
I like to taste it first, to see.

Not by reputation.
It depends
on who's gauging it.

Medium.
Blank.
There is no term.

To keep it, to tame it.
It would believe it couldn't fly.

The granules
rest
on the feathers.

I don't think that could *prevent* it from flying,
but the feeling of the weight would stupefy it somehow.

14 [is needed by all humans for good health]

In every game, there is a best strategy
for each player. (See also: secret annex.)

Often these stressful experiences involve a demand.

A town in Ohio we passed through once.
This time I went back as me.
A town that had been built to test the effects,
but they'd gone to such lengths!

They wanted to know the exact location of the afterlife.

she: Are you listening? What are you thinking?
he: I was wondering…when the Bronze Age was.

15 [removes tattoos]

I guess I'd want to ask her if she's ever
actually around. If she sees
anything. Or has an interest.
And I'd want to ask

if she's all right.
If she missed me, or anyone.
If she missed her life.

I suppose I'd want to tell her everything—
but at this moment, no.

16 [seals cracks]

Are there things that we ought to remember? This is still our question.[11]

Headline, "the line at the head"
from which the world is made.
There are steps—
literally, stones.
Consider for example the pattern: Sunny Place.[12]
The names
are legible.

No one believes the amnesiac.
Her little story, gradually told.
It snowed. Children's voices
arrived, like a memory.
The gentle memory that precedes the annihilating memory.
"Were you always like that?"

Why is the house empty anyway?
No one thinks of it.

17 [make a mini-volcano from salt]

In the old days when they were getting salt—
from the Dead Sea, say—they didn't know about refining salt.
What they called salt was really a mixture
of salt and sand.

When the mixture was more sand than salt,
they said that it had lost its savor.
But really it was just a bad mix.
They could be putting mostly sand on their food. They'd say,
"This salt has lost its savor." As if it *could* lose something.
Though actually it had to lose something. It had to lose that sand.

In the box. The round blue box. The metal spout. The little girl. My grandmother. Well, she's connected to it. She used the box, when she cooked, not a shaker. Pouring the salt into her open palm, and funneling it then through her fist. I got that from her.

18 [moves muscles, including the heart]

Colorless, tasteless,
not quite invisible:
I have a lot of "how things began."

He has the watch but no sense.
We're naming what we know about the earth.
That our questions will not be answered is basic as salt.

Six openings to indicate progression:
take
stretch to
boundary
inhabitant
voluntary settlement
with the help of God

19 [will smother flames]

I burn it out.

You know how if you hold a magnifying glass
above a piece of paper outside, the light will burn it?
Something like that is happening to my clothes.
I used to think it was you.

There are different kinds. I never know which is good.
Then it comes,
and I have a little.
I start to get in a good mood,
almost right away. It's salty! It's kind of rocky.
It's not about the taste, it's the feeling.

You had to add the salt because the water
didn't have salt in it. So you could feel at home.
Otherwise—I think you could die in fresh water.
Salt water creatures can't live in fresh water. You know,
plain water.

No one asks.
They don't notice.
They don't mean it, but they have their questions ready.
Not that I would want them to ask, but it's surprising.

First I was so busy, then there was a gap.
Then I made a big dinner instead of not

cooking, and we ate.
And watched a program about science.

Tomorrow
we can clean the house, and then what?
Things seem a little strange.
Dormant.

I'm happy.
I feel that everything's unfolding for me.
There'll be something.

She's just there.
She's in the bed. She's got a blanket over her.

She's supposed to help me, but—
I might have to help her.
I have to protect her, she's asleep.
Some things have changed.

Let's hold hands.

How're *you* doing?

notes

1. Mark Kurlansky, *Salt: A World History* (New York: Walker & Co., 2002), 5-6. Reprinted by permission of Walker & Co. Copyright © 2002 by Mark Kurlansky.

2. Robert Hand, *Planets in Transit* (Rockport, MA: Para Research, 1976), 466.

3. *New York Times* headline, January 14, 2000 (article by John Noble Wilford).

4. Roman writer, statesman, and monk, Cassiodorus (c.490–c.585)

5. John le Carré's *Tinker Tailor Soldier Spy*, BBC teleplay by Arthur Hopcraft, 1979.

6. H.R. Malott, "Salt and Christianity" (www.saltinstitute.org/pubstat/malott.html)

7. Nadezhda Mandelstam, *Hope Against Hope: A Memoir*, translated from the Russian by Max Hayward (Modern Library Paperback Edition), 9. Reprinted with the permission of Scribner, an imprint of Simon & Schuster Adult Publishing Group. English Translation Copyright © 1970 by Atheneum Publishers..

8. "Mortal Elements: Pat Steir talks with Louise Bourgeois," *Deconstruction of the Father: Writings and Interviews 1923–1997* (Cambridge, MA: MIT Press, 2000), 235.

9. Kurlansky, *Salt: A World History*, 7.

10. (paraphrasing) Nadezhda Mandelstam, *Hope Against Hope: A Memoir*, 218. "Twenty years went by between the time of M.'s death and the moment when I was able to take from their hiding place all the poems I had managed to save... I could not tell a soul that I was only waiting secretly for the moment when I could again become myself and say openly what I had been waiting for..."

11. Avishai Margalit, *The Ethics of Memory* (Cambridge, MA: Harvard University Press), 84. Reprinted by permission of the publisher. Copyright © 2002 by the President and Fellows of Harvard College.

12. "Consider, for example, the pattern SUNNY PLACE... This unique place is not created by some arbitrary searching for uniqueness. It is created by the repetition of the pattern which calls for a spot in the sun, and by the interaction of that pattern with the world." Christopher Alexander, *The Timeless Way of Building* (New York: Oxford University Press, 1979), 151. By permission of Oxford University Press.

All but one of the titles in brackets are phrases that originally started with the word salt, found in *Salt: A World History* or at www.saltinstitute.org, the website of the Salt Institute. ("Make a mini-volcano from salt" was also found at the Salt Institute site.)

"Ye are the salt of the earth: but if the salt have lost his savour, wherewith shall it be salted? it is thenceforth good for nothing, but to be cast out and to be trodden under foot of men." —Matthew 5:13

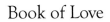

Book of Love

Learning the Language

Someone asks the name of your religion.
"Have you seen the canals?"
You and I walk up onto the platform.

Objects have names (what our dreams
come to). "It's what I want."
Begin asking.

"on the way to the ice"[1]

to run
I ran
my strong heart
through anything

as if each time we'd loved

desolate snake
the view was accidental

open the window
it's warm
we may be smiling
you would be exhausted
no beginning no end
when it breathes
it's safe
it's safe
this is good

our great danger
you know
because—no,
and yet—
of course

a safer place

gone to a better place
and such as: with my hand
in the fire, as Brancusi would say[2]

be more efficient (quiet)
more personal
I don't know, experiment
see the minute turn

break it on the way out

Complications from a fall

The moment she learned—

I'm thinking how she also loved the air,
crushed ice,
the wooden walkway.

It's a little long? things are missing.

It's the size
of a pea, that moment.

If we could
go there now—

reconstruct the room with our hands…

"You have to go to special places"
(clues)

"I thought it was for your eyes only"

Comes up kind of fast, would be a reason
to shrink from it.

"dead"
is deadly,

holding
the glass. The parenthesis

means something to me.
But so do the phases of the moon.

What does it mean to be <u>inside</u> the world?

The feeling that the room is open at the top.
(This white is my cross, as yours is black.)

Look up. What does it mean to be defeated.[3]

(You step from your skin, I'll drop my skirts,
and take your hairy coat upon my back.)

As it fell, I thought / prayed:
Maybe it won't break.

Loss of voice. Shattered glass
in our cuffs.

The river cracked. Time
isn't where it was.

"He's losing his frets." "I don't exist yet!"
He's losing his facts.

"They're not people."
Killing monkey people.
They all look like me.

I was supposed to raise the water.

But is it wrong?
If we let them, they'll replace us,
the fittest.

"The tendency toward conflict with strangers"

and that feeling when you're carrying eggs for everyone
and they always want to give you that extra
half-box.

Then aliens come

and take our planet
and eat our food
and talk the whole time about the better food they had on other planets.

As a plough opens up the ground to the sky
"things as he left them"

Arrive with something physical
and a list of questions

Everybody wants to have just one last conversation with the dead man.

Call before you dig
(keeps calling)

—Keeps calling the ashes the soapsuds, why?
—It's what's left. When the rest goes down the drain.

What isn't made from the impression: the mold.
Maybe not named.

The numbness
and the swelling,
the blood,
the rain filling the screen,
what connects us
to the saints.
Desire.

We could read the words with our hands.
"All are welcome through the eyes of God."

There are still a lot of letters out there.

Book of Love

"—then it turned into a flower. I don't understand.
It was a diamond outside."

Leave openings

for entrance from the street.
"That's why they have conductors"

(those big tubes running underneath the floor).

In art, like sex, the unbidden
and the willingness.

(the melting point the boiling point the melting point)

They call to one another.
Maybe communicate with flashlights.

("Nobody else can make one like me. And now I'm gone.")

:

Eros is tired.
Was a god,
is a moon.

"Arlene came home
with fifteen hundred dollars worth of gloves, and that was just one episode."

:

Crossed out:
Events here on earth.
I woke up.
are   so   I
We got wings.
Could somebody turn that down?

:

My vacation (reminiscing): Took a bath in brown water, cried for an hour.
Sat on the linoleum, read some poems aloud. In a place where the windows
stay open, my door is completely made of glass.

:

So much we say to one another isn't true—it's just the way it comes out,
so we need to be forgiving.

My father was alive and was becoming a draftsman. He still had something
to say about building. He'd lost something. That was important.

We'll carry it forward, he said, but separately. That same day we were
teaching ourselves how to think about life. There was a trick to it.

:

"It's more like windows—or pictures, in a row."
Recurring dream of a numbered list.

400: Introverts

(to be alone, to be with their animals, to think about science)

:

"She's writing all the time, and she's carrying a suitcase.
She might be going somewhere." (my temporary
girlfriend: strong stress, weak pitch)

I couldn't find the empty diamond.
Remembering together provokes doubt.

"for pitch is like light
and colour

stress
like weight"[4]

Scatters
the visible.

The diamond ring effect is seen just as totality
starts

and ends.[5]

:

The person in the room who never speaks, I was
(appearing,
disappearing islands).
I understand in 5 languages.
I understand you, try a little harder.

"It's the 2 kinds of yellow."
"He's pissin' pollen."
"Some people have pretty patios."
"Don't believe so much in the ground, believe in the bone."

Ideas: That someone could know you, without
doing the work. That you can have a second chance
at life. What people say: "saved for a reason."
(He thought I meant the lettuce.)

I was back in the old kitchen. We were putting the dishes
away. We didn't seem
particularly close.

"You might have to learn how to lie without leaving the body.
Put *that* in your book of love."

:

Ice, it gets under your feet.
You don't know it's there.
I was thinking of Keats, Baudelaire.
I was thinking of boys.

Why are we ashamed when someone hurts us?
Because it marks us, as valueless.

I can't hear you man
you're breaking up
I'm losing you

who goes above
so is this all up or down wander wander

to find love
to "find" love
to find "love"

no eye   (sewn shut)
pig iron   (saw not)

Can it be true that a lump of coal, under tremendous
pressure, will become
a diamond?
That a block of ice, as it melts, moves forward?

It was my father
who put the reindeer up on the mirror, at Christmastime.
Think of him

in the way he'd *want* you to think of him
(as every treasure
wants to be hidden first, then found—
the same with every crime, they say)

:

The 3 Cs ("like the 7 Seas")
Clarity
Contact
Commitment—
you can do it!
with grammar,
code,
the kind of stuff that washes up,
trash,
the kind you'd never throw away, you'd never have it
in the first place.
Blue plastic bottles, two, like
from another country.
From another time.

:

One, the creative.
Nine in the second place.
"In the third place, I'm seven."
sand / pretend
The papers and the piece of
green material—
I got them, I got out of there.

two
the receptive

water

"rock
and language"

progress

what conducts
what carries

red

our hearts
our diamonds

black as pitch

:

I dreamed I lived in a very windy place. The trash just blew across the kitchen floor, and there was nothing I could do about it. It was such a windy place.

Fragment. No suggestions.

Did she say who sought refuge
in unhappy love

Day by day, we're moving into night

Slight accent, and the falling
"Leave a window open"

"Which of these is life? the true life?"[6]

It's meant to be sad and bright, lit up
like the boat of the dead

I thought 2 hands would be 2 people

notes

1. "on the way to the ice." A phrase from a letter to Cid Corman from Lorine Niedecker. *Between Your House and Mine: The Letters of Lorine Niedecker to Cid Corman, 1960 to 1970,* ed. Lisa Pater Faranda (Durham: Duke University Press, 1986), 38.

2. "'My hand in the fire,' as Brancusi used to say." R.B. Kitaj, quoted by Timothy Hyman in his interview with Kitaj, "A Return to London," in *London Magazine,* February, 1980.

3. "What does it mean to be defeated." Agnes Martin, *Writings* (Cantz Editions, 1998), 69.

4. "...for pitch is like light and colour stress like weight..." Gerard Manley Hopkins, quoted in Susan Stewart, *Poetry and the Fate of the Senses* (The University of Chicago Press, 2002), 93.

5. Duncan Steel, *Eclipse* (Washington, D.C.: Joseph Henry Press, 2001), 11. [The "diamond ring effect" is the visual phenomenon usually seen just before totality is reached in a solar eclipse.]

6. "Which of these is life? the true life?" Paula Modersohn-Becker, *The Letters and Journals,* ed. Günter Busch and Liselotte von Reinken (Evanston, IL: Northwestern University Press), 152.

Where's the Body?

informant

"Begin with who was killed and why."[1]

If $x = x$,
$y = x$,
$abc = x$, etc.

salt for salt
ice for ice

If someone asked, you wouldn't call it pain.

Sound of rain, the water boiling over.
"one chance"

I lost my timeline.

Now that it's broke, turning black, something ticking in the closet (the snow kept it quiet for a while)

"That wasn't love—it was longing."

Everybody has ten days.

dusting for prints

The subject is distant from and dark.
The subject is seen through glass.
The subject reflects, or has a luminous body.

If you feel you can no longer pray, care less, don't be selfish.

Was he an artist?
I remember him cutting a sword out of wood, and painting it gold.
"Arms" seems wrong. It's their nearness.

Sometimes it's you and I'm calling to you but I say the wrong name.

Several glass ashtrays, the panther lamp. The light
bent toward the map. I spent a long time under the table, learning
to recognize wires. How we would change her.

How the bullet is scraped as it moves through the barrel.

The subject is distant, and dark.
Each instance has its rewards. Sex can't explain it.
"Their goal is to empty themselves."

If you feel you can no longer pray, personally, I like trees, birds.

Personal & unintelligible, my addiction bores me.
We still need spoons, plates, and knives. Bowls. Your star sign.
Those weeks with you?

I remember driving you somewhere. Driving, and it was snowy.
Nothing was figured out.
You said redemption looked like a painting of fire, after a fire.

Where's the body?

Things got complicated.
"It's hidden
in the ordinary."
(a shot that everybody
had
and used)

She said the locket hair was
"alive as yours."

Ate a teaspoon of plain dirt a day.
Changed her name to save her life,
to
deepen the channel.

Reeds pushed up by waves. Something about the way the junk is
pushed around, and left. Suspicious trash. (but it happens
all the time)

The visualized
bones
are unremarkable.
Yet, the idea: "earned the right to speak."
(a line that moves through the landscape, footage from before)

The silhouette
is within normal limits.
We perched, watched them dumping
the rock. Is bone
a kind of rock, were we rocks first? (someone said)

He dropped me off, he picked me up.

Things got complicated when we started to walk upright (you know,
the constant threat of falling).

plaster cast of a tire track

I was wondering if you'd like
this "memory foam."
So you can be more comfortable.

If we remembered,
who knows what we'd see.
I would be surprised to be who I am.

Should have seen him off.
I was repeating,
"black as a wig."

They have the barking
machine on. Flip it to Random.
There is no position. What—

secretary to a lamp?
to a train?
What I'm working on now,

big open book. Have you seen
how the root grows nut brown,
black as a wig.

wearing a wire

Someone would
have the feeling
something
isn't quite right.

The architect goes to a dinner party at the home of his former teacher.
Usually there's a small community: a boarding school, or a seaside town.
An outsider arrives who precipitates the crime, or tries to solve it.

There might be a group of people who meet every year at a summer house.
All that nature. A single mouthful can kill a man.

There was some problem—with his check, a problem
with the money. Something he wants to do
can't be accepted. Often there's a former life.

The weekend manager tried
to sort it out, but she couldn't. The lines backed up.
The guy behind me said stuff like this always
happens to him.

The trouble comes from keeping a secret, after the time's passed.
We have determined it's not about hunger. There is no body.

I was lying, I want you to see me.
I was lying
awake, something woke me.

I was thinking: I want to make
a few little changes.

The results were enticing.
It's a full life, collecting signals.
I understand support as: it fills in the gaps.

You have to fight the idea it should be
cleaner, easier, natural.

self esteem
self control
self belt
(She looked so different in her real clothes.)

self defense
He said again: I'm a jinx.

accessory

How many times can you bang one small body,
he said, and have it not
be a form of torture.

Up a lot last night—waiting for the pain
to move. With the now discredited
fever, "traveling fever."

When you notice that huge
parts of your
life

are missing. I made it out of what it looks like.
Ivory black, lamp black, mars
black, words from a book.

He's gone to Rome, it's his favorite city.
I call it "my black velvet"—that
day. That night, or day.

safe home

the subject
admitted
at that time
observation
stress apparent

flutter
in the attic walls

morgue type
gurney at the scene
they only want a peaceful life
can enter anywhere
soft skulls
palmprints

postraumatic
stated that the subject
cannot lift off

heroin cocaine marijuana
further history
unknown
unresponsive
marital status
unknown
in the third part of the night
weightless

not straight up
became unresponsive
swooping
without success
open hinges
must
fall to glide
glide to rise

I want you to see me

A crime had turned me into a phone. I tried to get sympathy from Michael but he thought it was funny. It hurt to laugh, but I had to. My receiver was transparent. I kept saying but Mike, I'm a *phone*. (I was still a person, in a way. I still had my legs.)

It was on the level of having a terrible deformity, or only one purpose (and not one I chose). I wanted him to care, but he was being so Mike. There was a flag or something patriotic on me—imprinted, near the dial. Red and blue and the white of my transparency. I couldn't even be a regular phone.

due process

She calls me to talk about
"what we have"—she calls it "feelings."
Blind for 3 weeks.

We have this: She knew my mother.
Uncross. The tiny click
of the turned-down answering machine.

This note
in a book: *No switch.*
Never tell the truth.

You tell me:
It's all about the shotgun.
All the breast feathers of a hawk.

Holding Basquiat's hand
as my teeth were falling
from my mouth.

So little
pain really.
Just open up, and let them fall.

eyewitness

The evidence remains uncovered.
Nothing taken. Dullness

and other signs of aging. "To be the center
of attention, in such a place."

Then a pattern of shadow, or—tar,
it could be. Bone black, carbon

black. People don't have
power, not now. Not of dreams

fulfilled. "Salt and tin foil."[2] The accident
avoided, but: "Everybody was so real."

being followed

Years passed.
I looked back to see.

Answer the following questions with yes
or no or no one knows.

I had a small and frightening pain.
Aunt Patty called, in love with another dead guy.

Wrong number.
I regret our
bus routes
Our hidden drawer
Our off in the fog on foot

There were all these choices, these different *kinds* of people.
Who to kill, and
who not to kill.

the welders
the burners
Seeing the pictures behind the pictures.

Civil war
Ghost
Leopard
In my heart, I'm free.
But it's so secret.

phone tap

Where nothing was, it had to be created.
We can't make everything we need inside.

I was looking for a sound. The energy called "drive."
Almost peaceful. But—how are you?

your foot?
your black and whites? your "prose"?

(I prescribe it for myself sometimes.
Where else could I find this kind of radio?)

disappearing ink

It's quiet lately at the fortuneteller's.
To control content, use actions.

"X"—someone who
hasn't appeared yet, but

whose purpose we deduce.
I know it's there.
Love, I think.
Or maybe it was goodness.

So many hopes for the outside.
(O hunger, O equivalent)

I approach it calmly.
It spills into everything.

conviction

Nobody has ever been so happy.

the city covered in snow
the town buried
"all rise"

"Only if it changes everything."

I know he's good—
(or) he's someone I love.

The freighter represents history,
the river is the ground.

snow on your coat

fishermen
reporters
police

He's still walking away.

notes

1. From *You Can Write a Mystery,* copyright © 1999 by Gillian Roberts. Used with the kind permission of Writer's Digest Books, an imprint of F+W Publications, Inc. All rights reserved.

2. "Salt and tin foil" (said to be the taste of blood).

Diplomacy

eclipsed

ordinary sunlight

what heat
reveals

crash-prone
first bite
bright stuff

to acquire the sun

the crest
the ridge

a part of life called disappointment

look for the break
it's enough

glow brightly in a vacuum

I think we have that, don't you?
it's green

and
it's unpredictable

prominence

to explore the sun
just   sit   back

it's working
it's running

aroused a demand
raised fears
this trace
let's go

24 stop

Clearing

He loses ground building cabins.[1]
The air reminds her of before.
People keep arriving (you, like all others).
We want to show you who we were.

Start by sitting in a comfortable position.
Notice it's powerful, yet pleasant.
One small room, wooden floor, favorite window.
The leaves are burning. Why should it be better.

If water covers the road

It's something about living on a former
airforce base in winter
in the desert, after they've all gone.

You can't help thinking of them during the days.
Going out or coming back,
waiting. The soldiers.

They're everywhere, and mostly
I don't know their names.

I asked a man in the hardware store for help.
"The only thing you want
to remember," he said,
"about the dead

is that the bottom
of everything is theirs.
The bottom of the river, the bottom of
every drawer.
If water should cover the road,
the bottom of that puddle belongs to them."

We're in the midst of letting go.
Knot by knot,
finger by finger.

Becoming one
of the three or four people
we might have been.

You can't always walk away.

"You can think about it," he said, "but
don't believe in it: on the earth
already means under the sky."[2]

Bridge

Watching a movie in which I'm in a hospital, being experimented on. They tell me it's like a dream (my idea, that I'm being experimented on)— that, really, I'm blindfolded.

The blindfold is so light, they say I can't feel it. (This is part of the treatment.) But I go to the mirror and scream: "I can see myself!"

The doctor says yeah, that's a funny thing.
How you think you can see.

Where there is injury
Where there is doubt[3]
I am melting, or
being flattened by the peach cotton pantsuit,
the saxophone
saved for a new life,
turned into cash

Stopped
to learn what is meant by:
a nice ass (braying) good
sex (boiling) liquid hours (stirring
with an iron bar, eating from your hand)

Stopped
to read a few things
from: the file Ideas / Old Dreams

(his "eye" unseen,
the particular valuelessness
of a dead man's eyeglasses,
contact lenses)

Where there is despair
"Since the first log fell across water"[4]
it happened like this:

"Doesn't anybody have the *real* potato salad?" Wandering from one
(imaginary) picnic table to the next. The impulse to get <u>under</u> the table.
The answer, in a way, is yes.

translations

[1]

Paintings of mine burned
when my sister's house caught fire.
Others were lost, sold for drugs, ruined
when the pipes burst at the farm
and we were all so far from home.

You're in a place that feels familiar.

The sky is so blue and they're talking so
loud on the wires out there—how can I
sleep?

Sometimes after I've spent the night
explaining myself to you...

"Wow, this wire is huge."

"This is the new religion."

I believe he said: "At the end of the
tunnel, a light." I'd never heard the
expression.

What is tired will rise.

"Shit. There's a live wire in my bed."
("It won't hurt you," he says.)

I knew he was somebody from the future.
And I knew: I was supposed to know who.

"Were you always like that?" I say yes,
but later think: who knows what I was
like? (having just the usual handful of
mental snapshots)

"If you bring forth what is within you,
what is within you will save you."[5]

"radiant dust"[6]

Steel
has to be made
of steel.

translations

[2]

Next: the house

Here is my witness.

could be razed
by the time you arrive.
You could find me
sleeping on the dirt.
Underneath that blanket

"a whole new system of faith"

protected
by the boxes I brought west.
The silverware.
The farm equipment. [rust]

to suggest that something started
and then ended

Well, the celebration got underway. We
were all sitting under a very big tree and
had a lot of picnic stuff and other stuff of
ours around. They lit the cornfield on fire
then. Part of the usual ritual. [smoke]

to suggest that something started
and then ended

> So far, there are the dreams, and the
> longing. I fell asleep and I was telling her:
> "It's amazing, I know, but you could have
> another life."

That time allows us
to see what we were blind to
and to become blind to what we've seen.

translations

[3]

People were telling their earliest memories.

What do amnesia and building renovation
have in common?

Sitting on the wall up at the school.

We were where you stop and I begin.

"Boats broken loose were trying to get
in at closed windows."[7] (You covered my
eyes with your hand.)

"Standing at the screen door, looking at the
sky, who did we dream we could become?"

Met a friend, a woman that I liked. Then
it turned out she was the one I sometimes
spoke to in the supermarket, noticing the
soft spots in fruit. She gave me a key to
her garage.

When you fix up an old house, you have to
tear away a part of it.

Earlier I was a child, and my friend grew breasts and had to drop me. "Let's take a walk anyway," I said. "We can still have some fun."

Nice to see you again.

You said life

You said life is nothing but
a dialogue with meaning.
Our common language.

It won't be what you have imagined.
A man was hired to kill me. I knew.
We've been lucky with the weather.

"half missing"
"a simple disappearance"
Call it luck, in case we get to live.

My arm was itchy, I was starting to lose
feeling in my leg. The devil
is to be encountered.

You say amnesia
is different from bad memory.
Because it could dislodge the lie.

I think it helps if you're writing a book.
Here's the rain. Here's the rain
is a good title.

"the inner landscape"

We lived somewhere. I was out in the yard, I looked around. I thought, where are we? Where do we live now? I came inside and asked you: what town do we live in?

At first, you seemed concerned about me, but in a minute you said: God... I just don't know.

We tried to picture the streets, but couldn't get past a certain point. We couldn't get to a landmark.

We couldn't ask the neighbor. But looking at her house across the street I had the feeling we had lived there too.

I could see her kitchen floor. In my mind. What a strange thing, I thought. Why don't we live there anymore?

Why did it matter what Valerie might think? Valerie would never meet Mañuel.[8]

On the fence?—that's American Bittersweet. First they take your sugar, then they try to find out how much coal you have.

Diplomacy

Start with a word.
The proper
name, the letter E.

tens of thousands
take a stick
you must expect to suffer

Think of the miners.

hooded people on the move
things keep flying or falling down there
you still hear about them sometimes
trapped

The eternal city

the wet ink
at the heart of faith

aged
and stitched
Or paved, for ease of use

They have a word
for it: "with new water."

Keep anger—his magnificence, certainly.

(I worry about
ice, if we get it wrong)

They have a word for:
"without the shedding of blood."
Imagine anybody trying to boss me.

There's always someone
shouting up the stairwell
sick with the news
no keys

And if it's the father
coming back drunk

coughing up some black stuff from a hundred years ago,
it's okay

to be disappointed.

It provides some extra
space (the half life).
To dig a hole they used the antlers of deer.

The "E" on its back, burning

rocks in the cart, feet chipped.
Everything by hand.

No one likes this story so I'll get to the point.
(but what's the word?
think of something nice)

You read about people who have something else.

There's a wild donkey loose in the street.
All the dogs came out to the curb and stood together.
Quiet. Not moving, not barking.

The Purpose of Discouragement

Imagine a movie in which every five minutes there's a still—a detail in the current scene, or something from memory—maybe 20 seconds long. Call it *The Purpose of Discouragement*. Sometimes it really is the last time. The beginning, or the end, of nowhere.

I was visiting my mother in jail and ran into Perry Mason in the hall. He was with someone, maybe Della. He might have been my mother's lawyer. I seemed to be involved with him in some way like that, "getting to know him." I really laughed at something he said, something about colors and decorating. I thought (did I say?) Perry's got some Virgo issues. When I woke up, my stomach felt happy from laughing—then I knew what I'd do. But two days before that, I'd hidden the letter, and I guess that was the first time I knew.

. .

By the time I arrived, it was too late to see the lawyer. I found the house without trouble. It was so friendly and plain. The porch light was on. I went up and looked into the mailbox, and there was the key to the door, in an envelope. I got back into the car, and headed down to where I'd noticed a food store. I picked up some tea and milk, bread and butter, a coffee mug, a couple of lightbulbs.

The next time, I took the key from my pocket. I unlocked the door. Would there be furniture, squirrels in the attic? I switched a light on right there, which worked. The house was smaller than it looked from the street, old, clean, and almost empty. Because they faced me, I climbed the steep steps to the second floor, still carrying the bag from the store.

A single bed upstairs, in one of two tiny bedrooms. Bathroom with a big tub and black & white linoleum tile floor, "marbled," from another time. Downstairs an apple green kitchen, old (some cracked) green tiles around a deep double sink. Stove and refrigerator, white, from the slightly-rounded era. Formica kitchen table, red, and three painted wooden chairs, one white, two yellow. I almost expected to find food in the refrigerator, as in a fairy tale. But it was turned off and unplugged. I got it going, and put in the milk and butter.

. .

"Because of your training, you may believe that you have broken the Law." The longing has started. But one must look inside, instead (a voice said). Look in the place it comes from. Thick walls, indoor sunlight. A place to wait.[9]

Some days have gone by. I've been sleeping a lot, in the little bed upstairs. Barely stir from the house. Got some stuff from the store and the Chinese place downtown and called the lawyer's office from there, late, and left a message. I have no idea who I could be. Given the chance to reconsider.

. .

How familiar it feels. Not like it's my house, but like the house is my friend.

There's a slanted skylight in the center of the front room that the late morning sun shines into—and I sit beneath it lately, since the rain stopped, in a lawn chair covered with a blanket. Brings it back, somehow—TB sanatorium, shipboard romance? Sometimes I drop off and when I wake up, I don't know where I am.

Along a length of two-by-four, near the site of some unfinished remodeling, a few bees, looking almost set there. Quiet, maybe dead. Or do they sleep. A somewhat rusted woodstove. "Oh, now this is the life" I was thinking, and maybe saying out loud to myself, as I picked up pieces of wood debris from around the yard. I built a fire the way I do everything: not quite right. And I felt so satisfied. To have the day, and the next day too. I feel safe here.

Funny, the sensation of freedom near water, when really there are fewer places to go. (In clothes, without a boat.) Bought a book a few months ago because of the word Ocean in the title, now I live on Ocean Avenue. Perhaps at one time the ocean could be seen from my street.

. .

Of course it's different when it happens to you. And Mary wasn't a relative. She was a friend of my mother's, from when I was young. A nurse, who took care of me once in the hospital, and rubbed me all over with a rose-smelling lotion. Her husband was trouble—why did she stay with him? She told my mother that she couldn't talk about it. Then one day she disappeared. It was shocking, and we missed her. We never found out where she'd gone.

I didn't forget her, but I hadn't had her actively in mind for a while when the letter came. I called the lawyer and discovered that she'd left me her house, no explanation, no special note. Had she heard my mother was dead? In the will she only said that she remembered me fondly and was sure I'd put the house to good use. None can tell more than she knows.

I've been walking around the harbor and the streets of the town with my camera. When I come home and download the pictures, I see the other town. The one I'm always looking for.

Found postcard: "I think the best part—the reason why we're here—is the lake. It's pretty round, a shape I like, a mile across. Now it's almost frozen. Even as I write this, I keep looking to the lake. We're very isolated here." No picture on the front. Who needs a picture. "It's not the romance of success, it's the romance of work."

. .

A long winter, longer than one season. Every generation needs a new biography. Down by the boats (After Hours, Endeavor, Almost Free) she decided not to worry. She decided that while she could she would sleep and eat and work when she wanted. She isn't sad, she's concentrating. How to face, or cannot face directly. What they call my coldness. Such a frightening dream last night. Going through my papers, I came upon my so-called voice.

flowering plans

Dialogue [2 doors]
may be incomplete.

The drawings suggest
"I have a drawing."
I seek the joy of living.
(They clap in time.)

His honor wanted to kill me.

"Your sons go out there
and maybe they lose an arm and it's great
but then they come home and want you to fix it."

[gaps]
There is no whole thing.
We know them all from someplace else.

Maybe the person you expected to die, dies, and it's shocking anyway. Or someone you believe has gotten free of her trouble kills herself, and you're sadder than you thought you'd be or, inexplicably, feel nothing. People always think that you could go away, to a new town, "just get on a bus"—maybe stay at a small hotel in the desert and write. And meet the locals.

Some people can draw a perfect circle. I was just driving cross-country, listening to a mystery on tape. Reading books in motels, losing track of the days of the week, a side effect of unemployment. You might not be familiar with this habit of mine, to relax when eternal salvation is at stake. Driving, I consider changing my name. Mainly, can't think of a name.

Outside.
If I want to speak of the fire—
is it close to you, or in you?
It's not "wanting."
If there'd been another way...
When there *was* another way, I took it.

The sun moves into my first house, and I experience a feeling of well-being. I don't want to be practical now. I want to be realistic. Getting the hang of the thimble. "The poet's needle." Only at the final knot, wishing for another hand.

You look for home and you land somewhere. You look for friends and find the dead. I picture these women as a chain of souls that I aspire to join. I have their dates up on the fridge.

New units of distance. In Berlin, the coral bracelet. For a future daughter. For a future. My rosemary is blooming. I talked to the librarian again. I know her car. Her mother saw the bombing of Munich. We met in the unexplained poetry section. Right now we're in the "getting free" stage.

Three wrongs don't help. She's got the iron down. Traveling with her jewel in the lead case, looking for a street: "Vale O' Tears," "Cat O' Nine Tails," something in that vein.

This morning, cooking oatmeal in the yellow kitchen light, imagining the luminous treasures spread out on tables at the lab. Spontaneously luminous.[10]

— How does "beauty is truth" work?
—"They neither toil nor spin."

Certain things recur. Was that plywood?
It was a strange thickness for a sword.
Just the perfect idea of a small sword for a small hand.

. .

A long day after a long drive. Some people I knew were going to my funeral, but I wasn't dead, I was just lost. This is the kind of thing that no one does on purpose. Seeing things as they are.

If our memories were scraped away, or just lifted from us, what world would we want?

Sometimes one person is ready. Sitting in weak sun. The lawn chair padded with an old plaid blanket, and me in his heavy woolen coat. Weren't the happiest days of our lives lived here? You know, sometimes a message from me may seem mixed. But do try to recall the idea that all messages join, somewhere.

notes

1. "He loses ground building cabins." Lorine Niedecker to Cid Corman, *Between Your House and Mine: The Letters of Lorine Niedecker to Cid Corman, 1960 to 1970,* ed. Lisa Pater Faranda, 37.

2. "But 'on the earth' already means 'under the sky.'" Martin Heidegger, "Building Dwelling Thinking," *Poetry, Language, Thought,* translated by Albert Hofstadter (Harper Colophon Books, 1975), 149.

3. "Where there is hatred, let me sow love; Where there is injury, pardon; Where there is doubt, faith; Where there is despair, hope." From the Prayer of St. Francis of Assisi.

4. "Since the first log fell across water, people have been fascinated with bridges and their power to bring together what had been separate." Judith Dupré, *Bridges* (NY: Black Dog & Leventhal Publishers, Inc., 1997), 6.

5. The Gospel of Thomas, Saying 70.

6. "They were all foreign and subtitled. Black and white and speckled with stars and radiant dust." Fanny Howe, "Au Hasard" (www.how2journal.com/archive/).

7. Rosalind Franklin, describing a hurricane. Quoted in Brenda Maddox, *Rosalind Franklin: The Dark Lady of DNA* (HarperCollins, 2002), 240.

8. "But why did it matter what Valerie might think? Valerie would never meet Mañuel. That was the remarkable part of being away from everything and everybody she ever knew. At last she could have a life of her own—completely her own—and do the things she wanted to do…" Betty Cavanna, *Paintbox Summer* (Philadelphia: Westminster John Knox Press, 1949).

9. THICK WALLS, INDOOR SUNLIGHT, and A PLACE TO WAIT are three of the 253 "patterns" described in *A Pattern Language,* by Christopher Alexander, Sara Ishikawa & Murray Silverstein (New York: Oxford University Press, 1977).

10. "One unexpected property of the 'new metals' had particularly delighted the Curies. 'We had an especial joy,' Marie recalled, 'in observing that our products containing radium were all spontaneously luminous. My husband who had hoped to see them show beautiful colorations had to agree that this other unhoped-for characteristic gave him even greater satisfaction.' ... Later, it would be this understandable pride in the luminous new substances which made Marie Curie reluctant to acknowledge their deadly potential." Susan Quinn, *Marie Curie: A Life* (NY: Simon & Schuster, 1995).

About the Author

Kate Greenstreet can be found at www.kickingwind.com.

Ahsahta Press

SAWTOOTH POETRY PRIZE SERIES

NEW SERIES

Ahsahta Press

Modern and Contemporary Poetry of the American West

This book is set in Apollo MT type with Goudy Old Style titles
by Ahsahta Press at Boise State University
and manufactured on acid-free paper
by Boise State University Printing and Graphics, Boise, Idaho.
Cover photograph by Max Greenstreet.
Cover design by M & K Greenstreet.
Book design by Janet Holmes.

AHSAHTA PRESS

2006

JANET HOLMES, DIRECTOR

CHRISTOPHER KLINGBEIL

ERIK LEAVITT

JANNA VEGA

ALLISON VON MAUR

ABIGAIL L. WOLFORD